How to Draw Foxes:  by-Step Guide

Best Fox Drawing Book for You and Your Kids

BY

ANDY HOPPER

© 2019 Andy Hopper All Rights Reserved

Copyright Notes

The material in question, hereto referred to as The Book, may not be reproduced in any part by any means without the explicit permission of the bearer of the material, hereto known as the Author. Reproduction of The Book includes (but is not limited to) any printed copies, electronic copies, scanned copies or photocopies.

The Book was written as an informational guide and nothing more. The Reader assumes any and all risk when following the suggestions or guidelines found therein. The Author has taken all precautions at ensuring accuracy in The Book but assumes no responsibility if any damage is caused by misinterpretation of the information contained therein.

Table of Contents

Introduction 4

How to Draw a Jumping Fox 5

How to Draw a Walking Fox 18

How to Draw a Magic Fox 31

About the Author 47

Introduction

Kids have this intense desire to express themselves the ways they know how to. During their formative years, drawing all sorts is on top of their favorite things to do. You ought to encourage as it boosts their creativity and generally advances their cognitive development.

This book is written to give you and your kids the smoothest drawing experience with the different guides and instructions on how to draw different kinds of objects and animals. However, you should note that drawing, like everything worthwhile, requires a great deal of patience and consistency. Be patient with your kids as they wade through the tips and techniques in this book and put them into practice. Now, they will not get everything on the first try, but do not let this deter them. Be by their side at every step of the way and gently encourage them. In no time, they will be perfect little creators, and you, their trainer.

Besides, this is a rewarding activity to do as it presents you the opportunity of hanging out with your kids and connecting with them in ways you never knew was possible. The book contains all the help you need, now sit down with them and help them do this.

That is pretty much all about it - we should start this exciting journey now, shouldn't we?

How to Draw a Jumping Fox

Step 1.

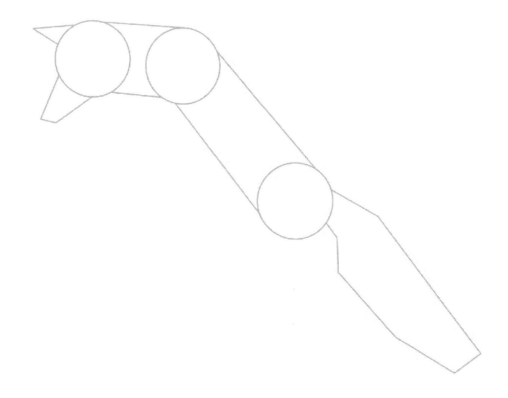

Add a circle for the head, chest and hips.

Draw the outline of the tail at the end of the hips.

Add a triangle for the ears and a rectangle for the snout.

Step 2.

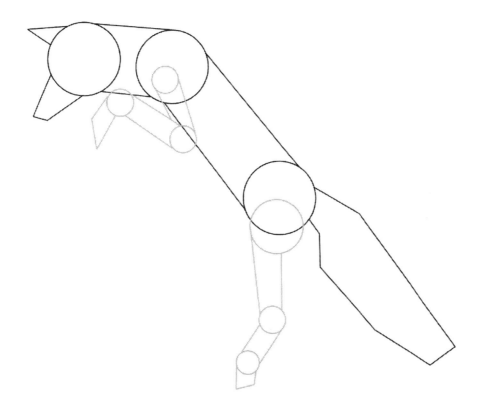

Add a circle for the shoulder, elbow and ankle for both the front and rear legs.

Connect them to make the legs and draw the outline of the paw.

Step 3.

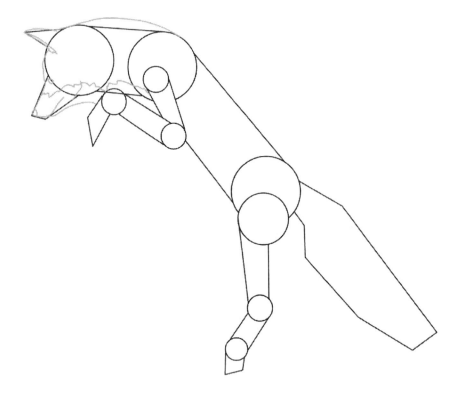

Let's redraw the head.

Redraw the snout to make it rounder and add a line for the mouth.

Smooth and curve out the ear and give him fluffy fur running from his nose down to his chest.

Use the example to help you along.

Step 4.

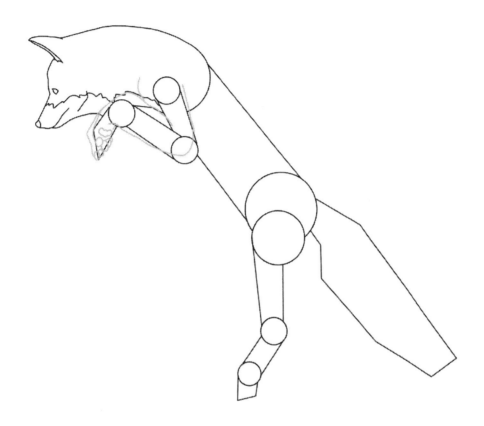

Redraw the front paw.

Make the fur that covers them and add the cushions to his paw.

His other leg is hidden behind the leg you've just drawn.

We only see part of the other paw.

Step 5.

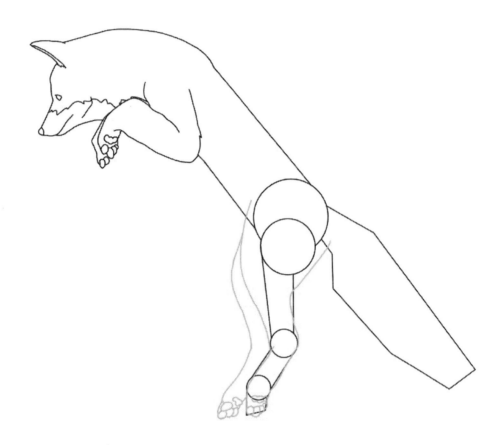

Now redraw the hind leg.

Give him fluffy coated fur with the cushions on the paw.

His other leg is partially hidden behind the first one.

Add the same curved legs, with the same soft cushion on the paw.

Step 6.

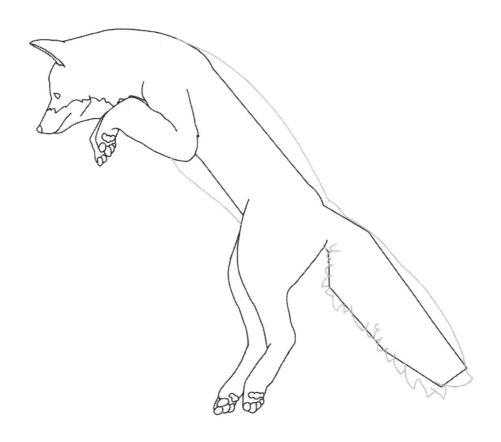

Redraw the body to curve and smooth it out.

Give wobble and a wave to the tail, adding fluffy plucks of hair on the bottom of the tail.

Step 7.

Time for some detail.

Add some fur to the ear to separate the tip from the rest.

Add fur to the paws for the dark part and then an additional line for the lighter part of his fur.

Draw the same line of fur down the belly.

Step 8.

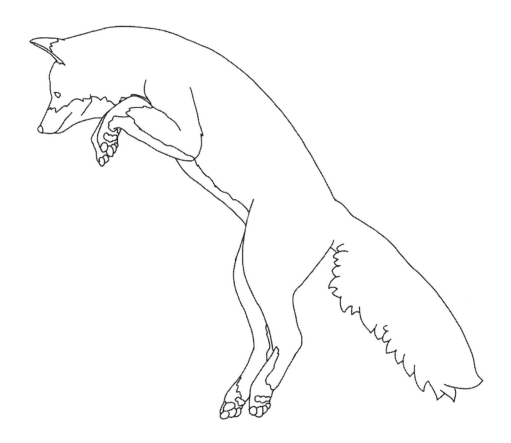

All done! Let's add some color!

Step 9.

The majority of his fur is light brown, with light grey for the fur on the belly, snout and paws.

The tip of the ears and the tip of the paws are dark brown. As is the nose.

The cushions on the paws are dark grey.

Step 10.

Add some shadow to give him more volume.

Step 11.

Colored version.

Step 12.

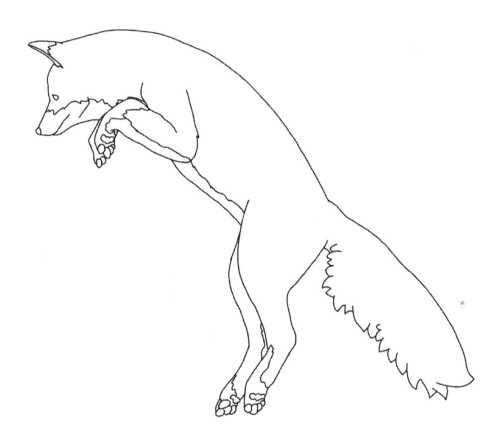

Line art version.

How to Draw a Walking Fox

Step 1.

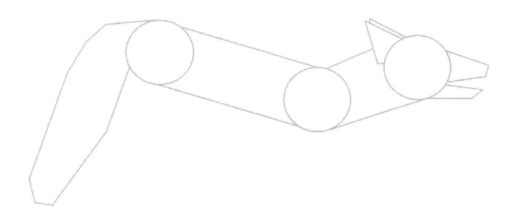

Add a circle for the head, chest and hips.

Draw the outline of the tail at the end of the hips.

Add two triangles for the ears and a rectangle for the snout.

Step 2.

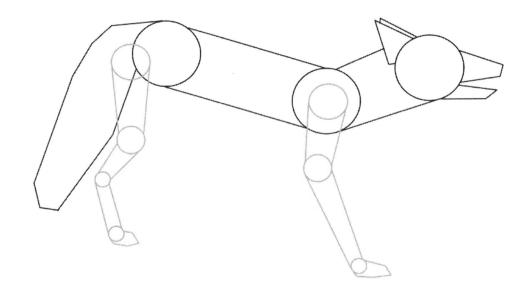

Add a circle for the shoulder, elbow and ankle for both the front and rear legs.

Connect them to make the legs and draw the outline of the paw.

Step 3.

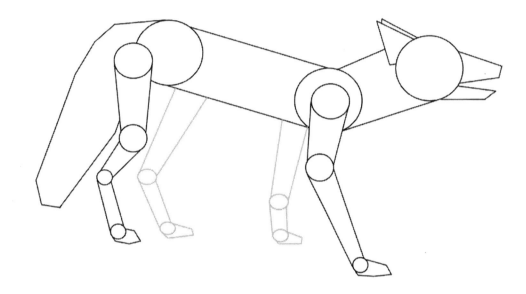

Do the same for the legs on the other side.

Use the example to help you along.

[21]

Step 4.

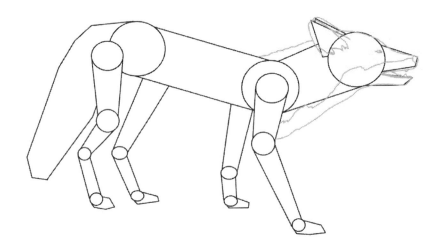

Let's redraw the head.

Redraw the snout to make it rounder and add the open mouth.

Don't forget the add the teeth and tongue.

Smooth and curve out the ears and give him fluffy fur running from his nose down to his chest.

Use the example to help you along.

Step 5.

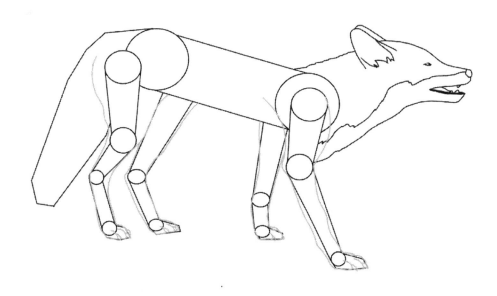

Redraw the legs.

Make the fur that covers them and add the nails to his paws.

His other legs are hidden behind the legs you've just drawn.

Make sure you add the nails to those paws as well.

Step 6.

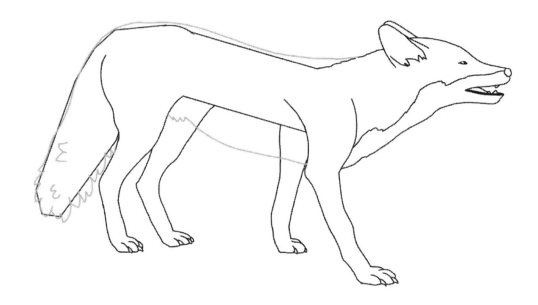

Redraw the body to curve and smooth it out.

Give wobble and a wave to the tail, adding fluffy plucks of hair on the bottom of the tail.

Step 7.

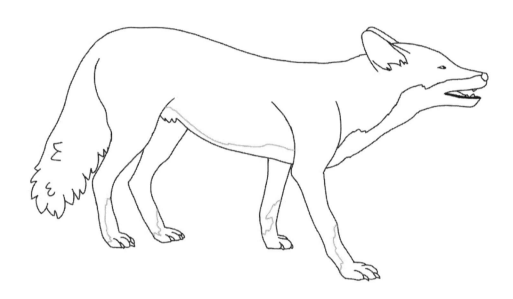

Time for some detail.

Add fur to the paws for the dark part.

Draw a line of fur down the belly for the lighter part of the fur.

Step 8.

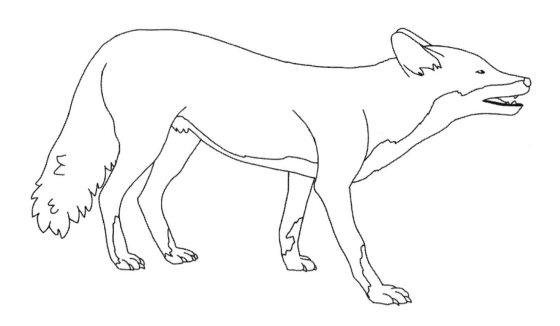

All done! Let's add some color!

Step 9.

The majority of his fur is brown, with light grey for the fur on the belly, snout and paws.

The tip of the paws are dark brown. As is the nose.

The nails on the paws are dark grey.

Step 10.

Add some shadow to give him more volume.

Step 11.

Colored version.

Step 12.

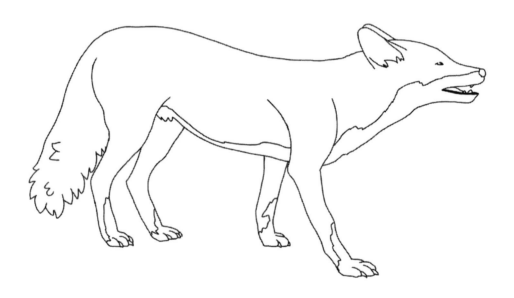

Line art version.

How to Draw a Magic Fox

Step 1.

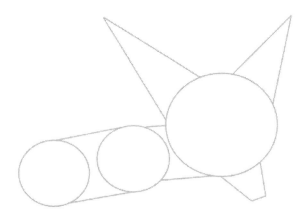

Add a circle for the head, chest and hips.

Add two large triangles for the ears and a rectangle for the snout.

Step 2.

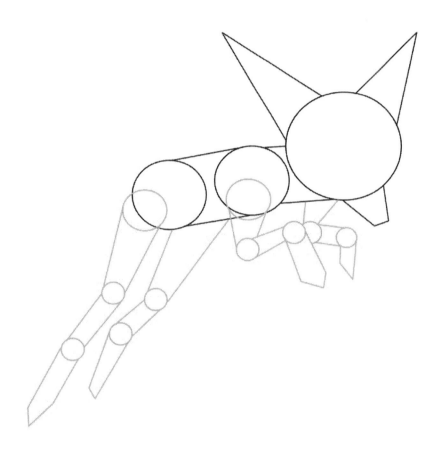

Add a circle for the shoulder, elbow and ankle for both the front and rear legs.

Connect them to make the legs and draw the outline of the paw.

Step 3.

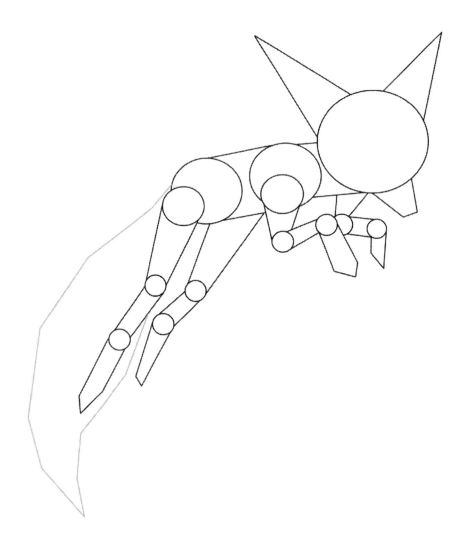

Add the outline of the tail to the rear of the body.

[34]

Step 4.

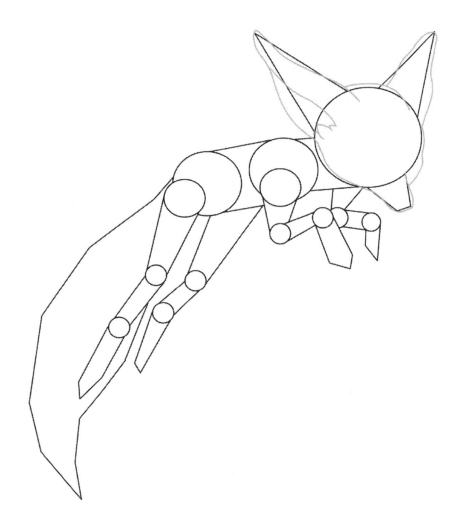

Let's redraw the head.

Redraw the snout to make it rounder.

Smooth and curve out the ears.

Use the example to help you along.

Step 5.

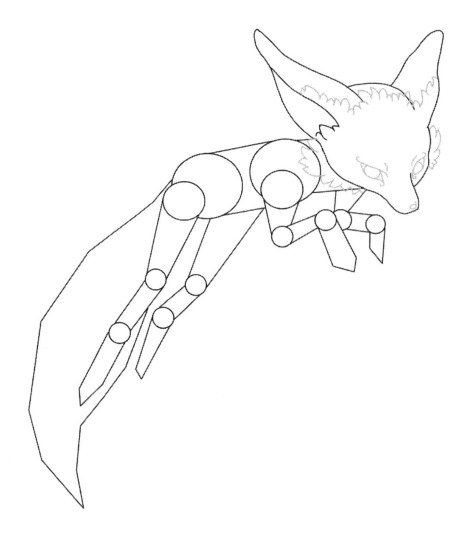

Add a ring of fur around the head, giving him some fluffy cheeks.

Add a tiny nose to the front.

Add two big eyes to the head.

Make his whimpers slightly whimsical.

Step 6.

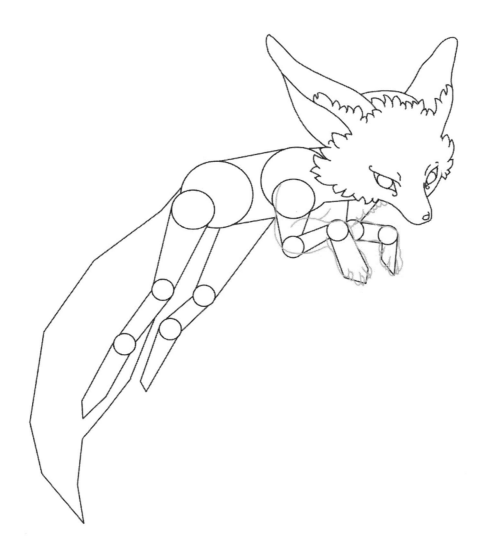

Redraw the front legs.

Give them a smoother form and add the nails to the paws.

Step 7.

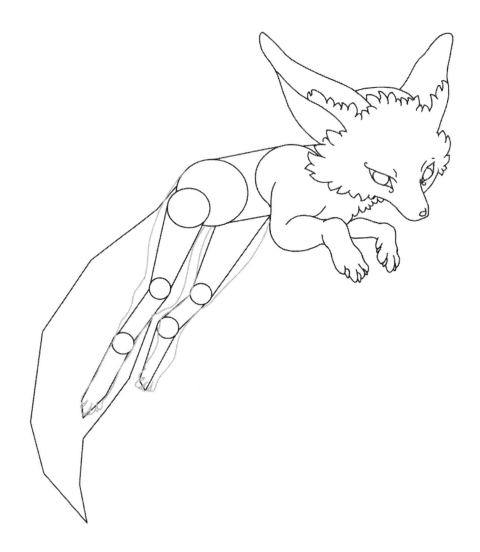

Now redraw the hind legs.

Give them a smooth shape while fully extended.

Don't forget to add the nails!

Step 8.

Add plucks of fur down the back and the belly of his body.

Then redraw his tail using thick and fluffy plucks of fur.

Step 9.

Add a second ring of fur around the head. Make sure to follow the shape of the head.

Add it to the ears as well.

Step 10.

Now add some plucks of fur around the body. Use the example to help you along.

Step 11.

Let's do some coloring!

Step 12.

The majority of the body is light brown.

The head is a darker brown and the ears are dark grey.

The eyes are dark brown and orange.

Add a dark orange layer over the light brown fur.

The remainder of the fur, as well as the face and belly are light yellow.

Step 13.

Add some shadow to give him more volume.

Step 14.

Colored version.

Step 15.

Line art version.

About the Author

Andy Hopper is an American illustrator born in sunny California just a hair's breadth from the beautiful Sierra foothills. After studying Design and Media at UCLA, Andy decided to try his hand at teaching his own unique style of art to novice artists just starting out with their craft.

He has won numerous art awards and has several publications in print and e-book to his credit. His e-books teach the beginner artist how to draw using simple techniques suitable for all ages. While Andy prefers using chalk, pencil and pastels for his own artwork, but has been known to dabble in the world of watercolour from time to time and teach this skill to his students.

Andy Hopper lives just outside of Los Angeles in Santa Monica, California with his wife of 15 years and their three children. His art studio is a welcome respite to the area and he has been known to start impromptu outdoor art sessions with the people in his neighborhood for no charge.

Printed in Great Britain
by Amazon